Holy the Body

Holy the Body

Poems by

Arthur Ginsberg

Cover by Shay Culligan
Cover Photo by Emiliano Vittoriosi on Unsplash

ISBN: 978-1-63980-082-7

Kelsay Books
502 South 1040 East, A-119
American Fork, Utah 84003
Kelsaybooks.com

Acknowledgments

The Anatomist: "Burn," "Microscope," "Plastination," "Returning
   to Kings County Hospital," "Skin"

At the Springtree Café. "Stroke"

Atlanta Review—Asia 2002: "The Anatomist"

Blood and Bone—Poems by Physicians: "Bill of Lading"

Brain Works: "Ode to Vision," "Requiem for the Paleolithic Brain"

Evening Street Review. "The Bones Are Singing"

Faith Is the Next Breath: "Paul Thek's *Warrior Leg*"

Floating Bridge Review: "Crossing Over"

How to Be This Man: "After the Heart Attack"

Jama: "Bogdan Vuksanovich," "Epithalamium," "Jerome"

Neurology: "Consciousness," "Holy the Hand," "Spine"

Seems: "Inviolable"

Contents

The Anatomist   9
Consciousness   11
The Butterfly Garden   12
Microscope   14
Epithalamium   15
Inviolable   16
Spine   18
Skin   20
Burn   21
Paul Thek's *Warrior Leg*   22
Farewell WD Clay   23
An Ode to Vision   24
Holy the Hand   26
Holy the Ear   28
Holy the Blood   29
Her Life Was a Concerto   31
Line Drive   33
Jerome   35
After the Heart Attack   36
Crossing Over   37
Sound View   39
Stroke   40
Bogdan Vuksanovich   41
Cirrhosis   43
Rictus   45
Plastination   46
Requiem for the Paleolithic Brain   48
The Bones Are Singing   50
Bill of Lading   51
Returning to Kings County Hospital   53
Holy the Body   56

The Anatomist

for my teacher, Martin Banfill

In this colony of bones,
he steps between cadavers
like a priest, benedictions on his lips
for the souls which no longer
inhabit these houses. His tapered fingers
guide my scalpel under flickering lights,
unzipper caverns filled
with flowers and serpents. He recalls

the prison camp near Shanghai
where he peeled the husks
from bodies punctured by bamboo,
enough holes to let the blood
run through like colanders. There,
he fell in rapture with cartilage and bone,
the way calcium wraps itself
in lamellae like rinds of bark,

becomes padded by muscle, tailored
in skin. He dissects from clavicle to coccyx
by torchlight and the rustle of rice
in the paddies, discovers how tendons
shackle tubercles, pull fingers and toes
like marionettes. He knows breath's end.
Death is his sextant
beyond the stockade's pyre. I study

his maps on heft of heart, pre-
ordained contour of brain. One winter
to voyage from pole to pole, to see
with Caravaggio's eyes, flesh's truth.

In this cathedral of bones he points
like a compass past supplicant hands
to anatomic north, each unwrapping
of skin with reverence, each body part
handled like a reliquary. Disrobing
of eyes reveals a celestial gaze
on the brink of another world. He
remembers his face reflected
in the pond of a soldier's last glance,
the sound of body bags
being zippered until dawn.
We are his disciples at the last table,
inheritors of priestly secrets.
In death he shares his humble skeleton
wrapped in linen, wills his body
to the pallet for dissection, an offering
to students of the human constellation,
exalted as the nameless soldiers
who gave their final gift to him
for resurrection in the classroom of war.

Consciousness

floats in the delicate
                    ether of butterflies,
brain spilt
                    into itself, warbling
through a garden of grey matter,
                    an unmistakable
interiority that does not emote,
                    gabble or quack,
is pre-syntax and babble,
                    reigns like a cloud
over the birth of flowers,
                    gazes across a moat
into the forest
                    of pheromones and photons,
the din of decibels,
                    and into the reservoir
of itself; a pool
                    of unshattered meniscus,
untouched by the tongue
                    that comes out of the mouth,
flicking the surface
                    like trout. Mind sifts
the presyllabic library
                    in every ridge and rut,
lifts on muslin wings
                    beyond the circuitry,
and waits for the anesthesia
                    of sleep, when consciousness
fibrillates, set free
                    to orbit in the galaxy
of Galileo's imagery.
                    Without it, worlds that men propose,
reality or dream,
                    would be unmindfully comatose.

The Butterfly Garden

*Like the entomologist in search of
brightly colored butterflies, my
attention hunted, in the garden
of gray matter, cells with delicate
and elegant forms, the mysterious
butterflies of the soul.*
 —Santiago Ramon Y Cajal

If not for Lord Brain,
who could have imagined

the nature of a thought
spun in its labyrinth

of Cajal's filigree. More
lustrous than silver,

and wily as a trout,
silent to the surface

before it's caught. Or re-
entry deep into the circuitry

where neurons that fire
together, wire together,

and etch their signature
in the hall of memory,

selected by linguistics
our predecessors taught.

And when, like petals,
thoughts unfold

and drop onto the lips, become
speech, become song, or

motoric offerings, 2 million years
of artistry murmur in the wings

Microscope

Peering through the thousand-power lens
I wander through a colony of white blood cells,
track their spiny membranes through rivers
meandering to every part of the kingdom.
Such intimacy, like embracing old friends,
endears me to this platoon of small warriors that rush
to defend the body's ramparts. Blue nuclei
float like seed pods on a lake. Inside these cells
our blueprints germinate, handed down
from creation's primordial flowers.

I am drawn to this labyrinthine garden,
its traffic through manicured corridors.
Beyond the microscope light assaults my eyes,
voices whir like locusts, the stark white benches
beneath tungsten lamps fade in and out of focus.

Epithalamium

The first time I ever saw a brain
all pink and throbbing in its ivory safe,
bulged through a hole the neurosurgeon made
to let the pressure out and so to save
my aunt who hit her head against a wall.
I was transfixed by curiosity;
that holy ordering of ridge and rut
fed by more tributaries than the sea,
repository for her every thought.

Hoping to find a grail of the mind,
I've searched the signatures of brainwaves
drawn from nerve cells shaped like tadpoles
in a microscope, watched patients seized
by toxins, tics and strokes.
The nature of a thought remains unknown;
what leap occurs between the ear and tongue,
elusive as chimera or a bowl
of sky that fills me to the brim, the brain
must be the bridegroom of the soul.

Inviolable

We know nothing of the secret life of brain,
even as it propels ideas onto this page,

only what essence evaporates when the nectar
of blood is blocked, or parts are excised

and discarded. If we could hike its ruts and ridges,
rappel down serpiginous arteries and veins,

nothing more would we know of the 3 pound
melon floating serenely in its sterile sea.

Cut it, magnify it—the mystery deepens,
as when a fox eludes the hounds. Shock it

to elicit a twitch, lobotomize, sever
its callosal bridge. Isolated from its five senses

brain withers like corn stalks in a drought.
At autopsy, this vibrant, pulsatile organ

wears death's gray cloak. Listen to the pathologist
pontificate, measure and weigh, pluck out a tumor

that rendered this human unable to recognize
his mother's face. There's simply no way

to interrogate what cannot be seen from inside
brain's domain—no way to take a head and spin it

in a centrifuge, hoping to float nubbins of what
makes it tick. Appreciate the cortical mantle

snug as the polar icecap, that presses the brake pedal
to control baboon impulses waiting like lava

to overflow. At war, clad in chameleon's skin, brain
barters virtue, enables men to batter, shatter, impale

without a shudder. Where will you take us
eons from now? Will our urges be purged or must we

remain cunning as crows? We revel in high tech's
genetic code, but the secrets of cerebral splendor

stay locked in time's strongbox, inviolable
and light years remote. Everything we are, the skull

contains—forests and oceans of love and hate,
the quest to delve beyond what is said, dreams to fly

to another place. Brain, teach us to love our unlovable
selves flawed as gemstones forged in rock, forgive

the carnival masks we wear that hold our worst
nightmares of stick men, at bay. By all means,

connect the dots, probe for the seeds, chemokines,
and stars hidden in this infinite garden. Ephemera

become more opaque as answers disappear into
questions, and questions erupt

in a geyser of laughter—something cosmic
that chains us to the knowable place.

Spine

you have held me in all matters
                    of gravity;
              extended, flexed and bowed

as a reed in the wind.
                    Between sculpted blocks,
              viscous pillows absorb

contortion and shock. All my goods
                    are hung upon
              your gallows, viscera

suspended like avocados from a bough,
                    the muscles stitched
              to a knobby rack, a ridge

like Stegosaurus, and dropping down,
                    the pelvis wed
              to sacroiliac. Bottom end,

vestigial bone of my tail. Perched
                    on top, the locked box
              of my soul. With Newtonian zeal

you have served my dance and line
                    with hubris and strut,
              priest of the bipedal romp.

There will be pain,
                    as my plumbline bends,
              white-hot Camellias sprouting

from ligaments. In time you will be
                    my memory
            when mortality's stripped off the rack—

you will shiver and rattle
                    through earth's cold prattle,
            the last witness intact.

Skin

Skin shelters us in cloaks of secrecy,
        pandering to private fold and ridge

with bristling hairs that rise from every pit.
        While at the borders of fingers and toes,

it morphs into cuticles and nails
        like leaves to petals. Menopausal women

camouflage their eyes with blue mascara
        to cover spidery disintegration,

while cellulite's nightmare haunts their dreams.
        Wheat germ oil, honeysuckle cream

mixed together in a thick mélange,
        applied like plant food to a golf course green,

will nullify the divots of peau d'orange.
        Impermeable, skin's our protective surface,

some scrofulous, some smooth like scales of fishes.
        But underneath we know no sweetness comes,

or honey to a pale, virgin peach
        without the character derived from blemish.

Beyond the covering that wraps all flesh,
        there is one epidermis we all cherish

that shields us from our earth's inferno,
        the crust upon which we have built our parish.

Burn

His face so terrible in the bus window's reflection,
you cannot turn away.
You did not know when you sat down
he would look at you as though to see
what flesh you are made of. He does not speak;
that hideous maceration of eschar,
crocodile scales, lipless mouth, lashless eyes
that burn like coals into your face. Outside
the snowstorm howls as the bus coasts down Cotes Des Neiges.
At night you're drenched by monstrous dreams
of icthyosis and thick-lipped crackling flesh. In the mirror
you stare at the fuzz on your twelve-year-old cheeks,
imagine the skin shrinking
into a shriveled mask across your face's
bird-bone precision.
In the morning on the bus he is there again,
and again you sit beside him.
For a week you do this impossible thing, until,
on the seventh day when the air is clear,
when he turns to you and grasps your hand,
and you see underneath,
something grotesquely beautiful. And he asks your name.

Paul Thek's *Warrior Leg*

Hirschorn Museum of Modern Art

Hacked off at the knee,
the calf of wood, wax, metal
and paint, sheathed by a leather thong,
glows with all its toes
in a Lucite reliquary. Weeps
for an unknown Roman soldier,
long gone, for the price paid

for an upright legacy,
its spouting artery
and shredded nerve. Once,
this was attached to a man
with a full set of bones,
who skipped and ran
and wrapped his legs
around a lover. Even now,

the artist's mind
lives in the shin's rosy shine,
as if he had been there
to catch the limb as it fell
from its thigh onto the blood-drenched
plain. Sad, disembodied leg,
you whisper from this jail,
splay your toes with plastic nails against
the unconsoling light.

Insensate, now, the band plays on
to sate the bellicose throng,
for those boys who fought after Troy,
who can no longer march.
Their epaulettes still stiff with starch,
and stumps like meat slabbed to the bone.

Farewell WD Clay

Now, death's mask scrolls across
this dear man's face like some hideous
parasite from the other place. And, breath

a timid animal escaping from the cheeks
that weakly inflate and deflate, straining
to lift his chest, four limbs inert and mummified

beneath the sheets. Still, a beatific smile
plays softly on his lips, and in the final days,
as stoic as a man could be, you thanked life

as does a tree for all its seasons of brilliant color,
aware the sap would sink back to its roots,
and leaves would shrivel and fall.

O' friend you were a mariner who sailed
the roughest seas, painted your heart on canvas
like wind upon a sail and in words

that tacked and reached across the page.
May all pain cease now in the arms
of your beloved mate. O' grace of light

dear man, as your widow lovingly ladles
your ashes with rose petals into the sea,
they glimmer in that shaft of sun,

resplendent as your life, as they slowly sift
beneath the Urchin's hull to the ocean's bed.
Go gently now in the ebbtide

to heaven's open arms that wait, cherished
by those left bereft in your wake,
faces you will know again beyond the gates.

An Ode to Vision

Give way to the mechanic
who ratchets eyelids up like a drawbridge
across the skull's dry sockets,

the glazier who fires the frit
into smooth discs of magnification,
suspended by caliper, like a moonstone
in the vault of each iris. Because the eyes

are an umbilicus to the world,
tether us to the names we've learned
to call heaven and earth, oak and fire,
know then the parallax of vision's garden
and all its plenty:
> the bee, the Bob-O-Link
> and Hop Hornbeam,
> the Lammergeyer,
that magisterial bird coasting the edge
of your perimeter. Let nothing blind

the millimeter pinholes of your pupils,
as you peer into the gloaming
of a day drawn down to rest;
> a rowboat bobbing at dusk,
> the shining lemon of owls' eyes
blazing in the forest. Invite the astronomer

to marry light to your eyes,
and amplify the starcrossed rays
from the latitudes of gaze, to meet
midway behind the ophthalmic globes, there,
to explode in a caravan of imagery
that drifts upstream into the river-
bend's soft folds where the oarsman offloads

its cargo into your seams. Take heart
in Hyperion who hurls lumens
across the cosmic meadow, unveiling
Eos, goddess of dawn beneath the moon-
lapped shadows, crowned by swallows.
Sight comes with the brush
of pale fingers on feathered last,
life's first and last epiphany poured
through the waterfall of your eyes.

Holy the Hand

in bird-bone digits,
perched on lunate pedestal,
sheathed in the rosy glow
of cuticles and skin.
Each finger tethered by tendon
can curl to beckon,
go straight to castigate.
Tight as mortise and tenon,
a benediction
of rack and pinioned knuckles,
exquisite pinch of pulp,
square taste of fist. Holy the fingers

splayed in flow and form,
the Pieta's palms upturned
to pray, and manifold
in all the ways of caress,
punch and slap. Nuanced
on piano keys, with the sensitivity
of an armadillo's snout,
some clenched, others outstretched
as Michelangelo's. Holy the hand

in profligate freedoms,
dexterous bequest
of our mathematician.
Like a macaw's beak, tenacious
as its talons, mercurial as mimosa.
Prehensile in grasp,
the messenger of intention, and when
sight fails, becomes the eyes…

Holy the plastic surgeon,
       master of tendon and bone,
who rescues the shredded hand
       from a grinder intended for corn,
and like the Eucharist,
       consecrates a new finger and thumb,
strong enough to grasp a wrench,
       turn a bolt till this man's job is done.

Holy the Ear

in its curvilinear structure—
the pinna, that as a dreamcatcher,
sifts the decibel led air
for codified oscillations,
funnels them down its dark, waxen tunnel
that spirals deep into the skull,
to thrum the tympanic membrane
like a kettle drum, vibrating them through
the smallest bone in the human body,
to the cochlea coiled as a moon snail,
where sound is sorted into ponds
of dreams and memories—
a mother's lullaby, rustle of reeds,
a waterfall. And when the ear is deaf,
cut off from its symphonic river,
that world unyoked from sound
becomes a silent movie, as when
silence was the only sound before creation.
Holy the ear that hears
your quiet breath at dawn, the pizzicato
of a violin, the song of the sea
that forever sings in the conch.
And holy the elephant's ear that flaps
to stir cool breezes, the boxer's ear
in its cauliflower disfiguration, and the beat
of the blood singing endlessly in your head.

Holy the Blood

        in arteries and veins,
birthed by marrow,
        pumped by the heart
to illumine the skin
        with a rouge glow,
receive gifts from the lungs
        to offload in the brain,
then, blue from its capillary bed
        through Galen's great vein
to circle again and again.
        Holy the cells,

some white, others red
        that people its domain,
killers ready to flock
        to a breach in the walls
in defense of the realm,
        deployed like smart missiles
at the body's beck and call.
        Left to clot in a tube,
the cells drift down
        like fines in an unfiltered wine,
leaving life's plasma, clarified
        as butter, on top.

Holy the blood that drips
        from the savior's stigmata,
the blood of children
        that runs in the streets,
Passover blood used to mark
        Hebrew houses,
the blood of libel
        dripped from so many pens.

Vampires conjured in Bram Stoker's mind
　　　　that sucked life
at midnight from all they could find.

Holy the surgeon,
　　　　who cauterizes a wound
through which blood runs
　　　　like a crimson tide,
the phlebotomist
　　　　who transfuses a man
to stop his essence from leaking away.

　　　　And holy the song
blood sings today,
　　　　a silent chorus in my ears
that gives me the vigor
　　　　by which to live,
and passion that flows
　　　　all the days of my years.

Her Life Was a Concerto

in memory of Jacqueline Dupres

Pizzicato

The sound is in the varnish, says the teacher,
laying the ancient cello at her feet.
He is a breathing thing with a slender neck,
strings, tightly strung across a resonant chest,
the high sheen of his skin reflecting back
to her, a freckled brow and glacial eyes.

For those tender years, he is the passion
between her legs, attentive to every pluck
and stroke, her lips curved as the scroll
which shapes his head, where tightening
controls the thickness in his voice.

She does not mind that he stands like a heron,
on one leg. With time, her fingers learn to fly,
deftly as a skylark, to press his tender vocal cords,
feel them press back, to make him come
in a tumult of notes, then, a little *pizzicato,*
as if to say, *let us frolic for awhile in the daffodils.*

Fortissimo

But for all his sonority, there is not enough
to fill her, so she fucks her sister's husband,
taking him in rapaciously, reaching around
to measure the distance between hard knobs
of his spine. Sweet sister Hillary; they
grew entwined as Siamese twins, one spirit
running down the beach, warmed one another
on cold nights and brushed each other's hair.

The man who weds his keyboard to her cello
cannot appease her soul that has already flown
and entered into the cello body like a sinner come
unto Christ, and taken into the grain of his wood.
London, New York, Madrid, Rome:

She's playing Elgar's concerto. Where the notes soar
to touch the cheek of heaven, on the topmost rung,
where her fingers are pressed high on his neck,
suddenly, she's wet. A outrageous puddle on the floor,
the bow launched from her hand, *fortissimo,* as if God,
in a fit of pique, had stripped His own goodness.

Pianissimo

Now, fingers become tortoise-slow
across the universe of his neck.
Wheelchair bound, blind and deaf, she puts
her lover on the balcony, to die. His varnish
cracks and peels on a rainswept night. In the end,
a brutal thievery assaults her brain, each sacred cell
gagged down to *pianissimo,* then struck away.
In the end, Hillary cradles Jacqueline's pain,
the empty hull of her body. She has flown to Elgar,
to Mozart, the heaven, she has given.

We are robbed and to God, what can we say?

Line Drive

I had come from a dying man's room.
What I said spoke to the cancer
eroding his brain—how his right side
would become limp, he would slowly
slip into a coma. And I pointed out
the silver shadow on black film,
from the foot of his bed, staying
at bed's length from him and his widow-to-be.
Said too little, too quickly
for the quivering ears and lips
where death was digging in, and I forgot
to touch or be touched. Going home

I passed a schoolyard.
It was a fine day, the light scattered
in shafts on the dark brown earth
of the baseball diamond. Clover grew
in clumps by the side of the field,
their white tendrils pulling in the bees.
Everything was shouting, *hallelujah,
alive, alive!* A mother cat cuffed
her kittens into line, taught them
to balance on the schoolyard big toy,
old retreads hooked one to another,
swaying in the breeze. I vaulted the fence

to get closer to the game, when the batter
hit a line drive into the pitcher's stomach.
He dropped like a stone, but was in moments
surrounded by Billy and Peter and Rob,
the first baseman holding his head, his
sobbing, coaxing him to breathe, *you'll live,
it will be okay.* I knew then,

I must go back to the man dying
in white linen, and say nothing more
than the warmth of my hands on his.

Jerome

Thirty years later,
      I can feel the urgency of his leap,
circle of arms tighten around my neck
      when I walk onto the ward.
I have become Jerome's friend,
      and we give each ghastly bulge
on his head, a name:
      Mickey, Minnie and Daffy Sarcoma.

Each afternoon
      in the waning light,
stories about Sir Launcelot
      or The Ugly Duckling; his eyes
read mine for the meaning of courage.

At night I wait
      for his lids to droop, kiss his head,
inject the chemical cocktail
      into the iv. line. Sometimes,
in the gauze of sleep,
      he blinks and smiles at me.

Everyday the dying children
      rise beyond distortion, play
with the fervor of Jerome's hugs.
      There is no way to prepare
for the time I arrive
      and he is not there;

the stripped-down steel bed,
      a clump of hair
from his misshapen head,
      the ammoniac stench that lingers,
the children's gaping stare.
      The rage I never said. His jubilance
when we turned the page to a swan.

After the Heart Attack

he lay on crisp, white sheets, hallucinating
bicycle wheels, how each revolution
must come from the injured sack, fibrillating
behind ramparts of ribs. Caregivers' voices
grew loud, then faded like children's, playing
tag in a forest. Capture the Flag, had been
one of his favorite games. Pablum passed
like prayers between his lips. He thought this was
heavenly and forgot the texture of meat; predatory
instincts edged away to some archetypal niche.

Breathing became sprint—he recalled a cinder track
where lungs quit down the stretch and knees
pounded on like an automaton, as if, they no longer
required the blessed sacrament of air. Toward the end,

doctors spread his chest, glued a patch to the pump,
to revive this dying horse. Wire sutures trussed him
together like a Thanksgiving bird. Wrist and ankle
restraints, he imagined as bracelets suspended by
pulleys from the ceiling. At night, these lifted him
into air where he swam weightlessly, flitted brilliant
as a firefly between hard shafts of surgical steel.
When that battered fist of muscle called heart, finally
ground to a halt, he was soaring through the forest,
bathed in mosaic columns of light,
unaware of the crash cart's shock, listening
to the whole universe call his name.

Crossing Over

In her white paddock,
      the woman dreams a mare,
         flanks churning

to stay afloat. Unaware
      the distance stretches too far.
         Ten to twenty knots

on the inland waves,
      but a hard wind
         fractures the surface

Every day, shining water
      streams in rivulets
         across her back

foaming like suds,
      and the withers bunched
         in one surge

beneath all the swift torrents
      of felicity and faith,
         her mane fanned

like a wedding train
      for steerage,
         and overhead,

the relentless sun
      insolent
         to the bit,

bulging eyes, frothing lips,
      the mallard she passes,
            smoldering like an emerald

on the water's skin
      that breaks now like waves
            to drown

this struggle
      under tungsten lamps,
            the heart monitor's

vicious hum marking
      the end of her life
            in a ripple.

Sound View

Mr. Michener dies tenaciously
       in the hospital bed. Cancer
has eaten his ears to nubs. Stroke
       has pilfered his words. Eyes
brim with the justice of hemlock.
       Right hand flails
like a netted flounder, pulls
       the nasal tube urgently
as a deacon sounds belfry chimes
       in an emergency.

He cannot see the sound view
       from the misted window,
how water spreads like curls off
       the shore's chest, blood-colored
at ebb tide, distills into sky,
       rebirths from the plump
ovulation of clouds. He is not ready
       for the legend of white light
at tunnel's end, squeezes my hand
       in search of intimacy. Eyelids
droop with the effort of not finding
       words, drool puddles on his lips.

My mumbling dissolves on muffled ears—
       how can I know this passage?
When his grandsons arrive, a half smile
       plays across slack lips, death
molds his face, placid as the sea,
       break-watered past the spit of land
named Point-No-Point.

Stroke

comes down, brutal as an avalanche,
erasing the playground of speech,
piles up in a drift at the tip
of Veida's tongue. She cannot repeat,
no ifs, ands, or buts, calls a comb,
bone, pen, *cow.* Frustration bleeds
through her brokenness, shudders in
chaotic clutching of spindly fingers,
as if, the right word could be plucked
from air. *Veida, Veida, listen to me.*
Follow my hand with your eyes. Eyes
brimming, she nods and follows, pendulum
on command. Stroke pitches camp,

lays rebar, pours cement. She grows to
know me and I, her, without ancestral
gift—small patch of brain, ordered as
the stars. From bedside, touch speaks,
vision flows in syllables, unfettered as
a child skipping rope. Fingertips vibrate
loquaciously as lips, extolling all the hope
of eighty-five years—married to darling Jack,
librarian, rebuilding spines of orphaned books.

Stroke binds her in the vault of our audacious
builder, pitiless as, buried alive. I visit Veida
each day, stunned by peals of laughter
at her own infirmity, that come from cosmic space,
roiling up through ghostly cracks to pry open,
the lock. Waylaid by walls, eyes fade,
no word to frame, *goodbye.*
Undoing speaks to the marvel of design—
more eloquent than speech, the vespers of silence.

Bogdan Vuksanovich

At Interlaken, I push off on skates,
a rhythmic glissando across
the water's frozen face. Wind
works the high branches of the birches,
singing for sap's return. Earlier today,

I wore my instructor's cap, watched
Vuksanovich lurch from his wheelchair,
weave on sailor's legs to the table.
Medical students gawked at him;
a zoologic exhibit, *oohed* and *aahed,*
when I demonstrated damage according
to the textbook: eyes that ricocheted
like bullets, and ankles that pumped
like a startled deer at the stroke
of a reflex hammer. Signs of assault

on flowering brain, petals stripped
off matrix of tectum, tegmentum and pons,
weevils punching holes in hippocampus
and corpus callosum. I reveled
in this showpiece of pathology,
pulled out a slick word for impaired
coordination: *dysdiadochokinesia.*
They imbibed with zeal, pelted questions
like hardballs at a catcher. One student
blurted out, *can he get an erection?*
We were shamed. Bogdan retrieved a photo
of his year-old daughter. We admired
shining cheeks and tiny puckered lips.

By the boathouse, ice is cracked
and heaved, a tented jigsaw,
defiling geometry. What is broken
by nature is beautiful, creaks and groans
like human disease. I balance on one foot,
aware a slip could fracture bones.

Cirrhosis

Think of a palm tree growing out of your navel,
also known as the Caput Medusae, says the professor,

named after the monster who had hair
made out of snakes according to Greek mythology,

placing her stethoscope over the swollen veins,
so her brood of students can listen to

the Cruveiler-Baumgartner murmur, a sign
of increased pressure and blood flow in the liver.

Sweating under my white coat I palpate
with my fingertips, the cirrhotic edge of a ruined organ

that seesaws beneath this man's twelfth rib
with each inhalation. Imagine this human being,

eyes wide with fear as stethoscope after
stethoscope with cold diaphragms interrogate

his bellybutton, their reaction punctuated by
oohs & aahs, while the professor in stentorious voice

warns of impending catastrophic hemorrhage!
Did anyone ask the man his name?

We move on to the next bed and the next,
following and clucking devoutly after the mother hen

pecking her way through this labyrinthine ward
of agonal Brooklyn souls, delirious and hallucinating,

hoisted on their own alcoholic petards, some blinded
by aftershave lotion cut with wood methanol.

By midnight I begin to understand the meaning
of misery, the tawny color of livers

depicted in textbooks, the jaundiced hue
of bilirubin-tinged eyes. By midnight,

I come 'round to John Doe, hold his hand,
ask his name, the whereabouts of his children

and wife. This, before he suddenly gurgles,
clutches his throat and ejects a stream of blood that hits me

like a geyser in the chest—then he is gone.
I stumble to the dorm, thirsty for what might kill me.

Rictus

The men in white coats call it, *rictus*—
the death mask smile. They say
just a spasm of the risorius muscle,
but who knows what that grin really means?

Last night beneath a gibbous moon,
a cougar killed a deer on the lawn. Stripped
the muscle off its right haunch, strewed
intestines coiled like springs on the grass,
deflated lungs straddling the windpipe, but
her lips curled in a most beatific smile.

I remember the agony on my father's face
as cancer tore through his body,
and blood spilled onto the hospice floor.
Then, the letting go, his jaw unclenching
like a clamshell, into a prophetic smile.
Rictus, the nurse said, patting my shoulder—
just a reflex of the dead—but I imagine

he may have seen something we cannot know—
perhaps an image of my mother haloed
in sunlight, leaning against a birch tree, holding
her white terrier, Teddy. And he knew
he had found what lucky men find in this life.

Now, when I meditate, those sweet souls
shimmer before me in a radiant light, just
out of reach. Something, even a deer sees—
this other place, this infinity beyond
the savage night, that summons the last smile.

Plastination

Start with a corpse, the bluish
            monogram of *livedo reticularis*
    on its flanks. a whiff
of plastic polymer and formalin
            in the air. A little man
    wearing a black fedora
and the hieroglyphs of grandiosity
            cut into his cheeks,
    who promises to resurrect
your lover's body, pristine
            as Amenhotep,
    for a thousand years.
Vacuum the fluids and fat, force feed
            the arteries, like a goose
    for *foie gras,* with rubber that glows
like neon. Pack the muscles with silicon,
            inflate
    the blanched nipples. Bisect
the skull to reveal her brain—
            a pasha perched
    in the minaret of his caliphate—
its ruts and ridges
            glossy now,
    crisscrossed by veins,
as if, the love she lavished
            on you, was still
    contained. That little man
will slice thin sections
            of her heart, like ham
    on a butcher's blade;

a painting framed
              to hang in your mausoleum.
        Walk between the stainless steel
vats and jars on shelves,
              filled with bright remains
        from someone's gutted husk.
Ask yourself if Mozart's music
              could be any sweeter,
        had we, his pauper's body
to gawk at, in a glass case. Ask
              the man in the black fedora,
        why he seeks immortality,
what blinded him, in the body's geometry,
              to the weightlessness of dust.

Requiem for the Paleolithic Brain

Let me cauterize

with the surgical wand,
that limbic almond named, *amygdala,*

a brimstone repository

nestled deep in the brain's putty—
sulfurous nugget

of Neanderthal rage

like a sabertoothed tiger
fecklessly seeded by creation

inside our heads—

once I believed
that Sapiens was divine,

hairless inheritors

fashioned from the sacred dust
of whirling galaxies,

now weary

in our monstrous fits and starts
through clotted millennia,

castaways

in the two-by-two ark, disguised
in a thin mantle

of gray matter—

how evolution's gamble has hurt
our lives, spilled this unsavory rage

in fiery cages

        where smoke snakes into nostrils
        leaving blackened lungs

hungry for air

        in a cave of lengthening shadows,
        bat guano and silence.

We were hobbled

        in the steaming kitchen
        before we chimped across the savannahs,

delusional,

        we were in control
        of this vestigial bomb that ticks

inside an unholy spirit—

        tick, tick, tick...into an opaque
        dawn of spliced chromosomes

annealed to steel fists.

The Bones Are Singing

At Dover Air Force base, the Corporal
bends to his work with the focus
of a diamond cutter, drapes the bones

in the Stars & Stripes, pins the Purple Heart
to the casket's satin lining. Bleached bones
that were interred in a rice paddy,

found glinting beneath the starlight
of a summer's night, come home now after
thirty years, to a daughter not yet born,

when her father was called to war. Leg bones
that carried him into battle, arm bones
that would have cradled her, the perfect

tongue & groove joinery of his spine, scaffold
for the flesh, still straight and unyielding.
She arrives to honor him, the last and only time

she will meet her father. In what seems
an audacious act of grief, she curls her hand
around his vertebrae—adoration rising

from the macabre—begins to hum a lullaby
under her breath. Reconstructs in her imagination,
the man from these hallowed bones, the father

she knows only from yellowed photographs,
clad in camouflage, beside a helicopter. The note
found in his footlocker promising her to come home.

And everywhere, in far flung fields & forests,
beneath glaciers and deserts, ancient & contemporary,
the orphaned bones are singing…

Bill of Lading

Anton Steiner sits behind a rosewood desk
in the ivory tower across the street from
Armageddon. I stand before him, buck private
intern, drenched in sweat and grime. After
48 hours of emergency duty, he demands
a bill of lading; handwritten cards on seventy
Brooklyn souls in various stages of entropy.

I want to say I am fatigued and my feet ache, that
I don't give a damn for documentation, that
I want to sleep and shower, the way he did
before work. I want to say, the cards will not tell
Jose Martinez's story, how he died in my arms,
a chunk of steak wedged in his windpipe.

He is as impassive as dust, the metal
of his eyes, a glacial blue. He has forgotten
the feel of membranes, slick in a split-open chest,
putrefaction from an addict's abscess, the **all clear**
shout before paddles convulse an arrested heart.

The cards will not recall Dora, bag-lady from Flatbush,
who thinks I am her reincarnated son from Jerusalem,
will not recapture one iota of my pleasure when
I cut through Amber's pantyhose, to reveal
the glistening head of her newborn son. Or horror
of a man who penetrated himself with a lightbulb,
forgetting glass is fragile. I want to tell Steiner

that these cards are old news, the ink was spilled
hours ago, that the ink ran like blood to my knees
and elbows, that the world is strangling in ink
and paper, that neon patterns on oscilloscopes

are something we have invented to detach us
from matters of the heart. In mellifluous voice,
he asserts, *the report is due by nine, your future
depends on it, that is all.*

Returning to Kings County Hospital

In these sprawling wards, on beds
sheathed in coarse linen,
I learned to interrogate the heart,
to know the opening and closing valves,

hold an ear to the lungs for rales and rhonchi—
signature sounds of a drowning chest,
to palpate with fingertips, a knobby liver
beneath the ribs, hard as a hickory gall.

To spelunk the body's caves
by headlamp and touch, to see beyond
the eye's pinhole, serpentine rivers running
and the ivory cable carrying the world

into the brain's rutted ridges.
On that journey I became a warrior
armed with the staff of Asclepias, bound
by Hippocrates' oath, the serpent growing

new skin entwined around my feet.
I took with me to New York:
the prying ear of a stethoscope,
a white jacket and name tag, the child

inside me who died on the fever's
battlefield. I carried my ashes in an urn,
and joined one hundred and ten interns
in the contagious corridors

of old Kings County Hospital standing
in Brooklyn's blazing desert. Graffiti crawls
its walls like ivy, and the wagons arrive
screaming with their cargo of wounded.

On Flatbush Ave. the sick pile up
on steel gurneys stacked like boxcars:
in a stockyard. *We are cattle,*
Help us to die. And I press

against the nursery glass,
drinking in the puckered, red faces
inhaling life, the bubbles on tiny lips.
Years ago, I drove through Brownsville,

a graveyard of fractured walls,
pitted asphalt and shattered windows.
I ran red lights, looked away
from dark figures warming their hands

over can fires. Their faces vibrate
before my eyes, black as coal miners
pulled from a pit. Misery gathers
this world's dead weight on their backs.

Each night, more babies with cigarette
burns, the elderly, gaunt and cold.
The Lindens' leaves on the boulevard
have turned from gold to red.

No sleek, black monument honors the dead
on Flatbush Ave. where the old men
in the park are fed by the pigeons,
where I worked in a place

where human life had a diminished
meaning, where the hopes of the hopeless
are cast adrift. Lowell said,
        the elected who promise to care,

come here bright as dimes,
and die disheveled and soft.
My mother arrived in a hard snow
to scour my room in the dentist's office

where I lived, and brought freshly
laundered clothes. In this wasteland
she shone like a beacon, left a spotless
windowsill, this tidied room,

the orchestral bedsprings, anatomy books,
a goose necked lamp and vitamin pills.
In the autumn I wander Kings County's
corridors again, searching for Miss Sardi,

the Sicilian nurse who tested my mettle,
blocked my exit from intensive care,
with mellifluous voice demanding the name
and dose of a drug for Pedro Martinez,

a dying man assigned to me on my first day.
I relive a chorus of respirators sucking air, red
diaphragms rising and falling in glass cylinders.
The usual, I blurted out, bolting through the door.

An orderly informs me that she passed away.
From the deck of the Staten Island ferry,
my life leans toward a kinder season,
Ellis Island fading in the mist.

Holy the Body

in intricate design
        sheathed in skin
assembled on bone
        the spine on which
all else is hung
        a jigsaw marvel
of groove and tongue
        its central canal
a conduit for
        the power cable
to body and limbs

And holy the tendons
        anchored to joints
that pull the muscles
        like marionettes
to leap and sprint
        sheer joy in motion
up mountain on water
        embracing exhaustion

Holy the lungs
        translucent as squid eggs
that capture oxygen
        from air
the heart that endows
        most tender hours
or rages when men
        usurp its power

And holy the liver
       that hides like a possum
beneath a rampart of ribs
       to recycle waste
spilled into the blood
       almond shaped kidneys
that filter toxins
       through filigreed webs

Most holy the brain
       in its ivory tower
that sees and hears
       feels and tastes
the conductor
       of this orchestra
waving its baton
       over all we think
over all our actions
       laughter and tears

Holy this body
       constructed of flesh
and sea
       what a piece of work
that serves us endlessly
       more reliably than
the cogs and gears
       of machines made of steel
this body that lasts
       for a hundred years

Praise the body
       broken and sound
with all its mysteries
       and imperfections
through millennia
       it honors its crown

Durable as I am
       handle me with care
and when decay has come
       and the splendor I was
has flown
       return me to earth's cradle
and keep my memory
       for as long as
I'm warmed by the sun

About the Author

Arthur Ginsberg is a neurologist and poet based in Seattle.

He has studied poetry at the University of Washington and at Squaw Valley, with Galway Kinnell, Sharon Olds, and Lucille Clifton. Recent work appears in the anthologies *Blood and Bone* and *Primary Care* from University of Iowa Press. He was awarded the William Stafford prize in 2003. He attained an MFA degree in Creative Writing in July 2010 from Pacific University in Forest Grove, Oregon where he studied with Dorianne Laux, Marvin Bell, and David St. John. His book, *The Anatomist,* was published in the summer of 2013. A second book, *Brain Works,* has been recently released by David Roberts Books. He currently teaches a course titled "Brain and the Healing Power of Poetry" at the University of Washington.

www.ingramcontent.com/pod-product-compliance
Lightning Source LLC
Chambersburg PA
CBHW021027090426
42738CB00007B/926